Mr. Whisk

Written by Claire Daniel
Illustrated by Rosekrans Hoffman

It was time for bed.
Mr. Wink fell asleep.

HOOT! HOOT! HOOT!

There was the sound of an owl.

Then Mr. Wink woke up.

Tick tock. Tick tock.
Mr. Wink fell asleep.

TAP! TAP! TAP!

There was the sound of the rain.

Then Mr. Wink woke up.

Tick tock. Tick tock.
Mr. Wink fell asleep.

BUZZ! BUZZ! BUZZ!

There was the sound of bees.

Then Mr. Wink woke up.

"I wasn't able to sleep a wink last night," said Mr. Wink.

"So tonight I'll use these!"